D1457902

ALSO AVAILABLE IN
THE WISDOM OF SERIES

ANCIENT GREECE
Compiled by Jacques Lacarrière
Photographs by Jacques Lacarrière

ANCIENT ROME
Compiled by Benoît Desombres

BUDDHA
Compiled by Marc de Smedt
Photographs by Jean-Louis Nou

ISLAM
Compiled by Nacer Khémir

JESUS
Compiled by Jean-Yves Leloup

JUDAISM
Compiled by Victor Malka
Illustrations by Marc Chagall

ZEN
Compiled by Marc de Smedt
Calligraphy by Master Taisen Deshimaru

THE WISDOM OF
TAO

Compiled by Marc de Smedt

Abbeville Press   Publishers
New York   London   Paris

Cover illustration and vignettes by Danielle Siegelbaum

For the English-language edition
RESEARCH, TRANSLATION FROM THE FRENCH, AND BIBLIOGRAPHY:
John O'Toole
EDITOR: Jacqueline Decter
TYPOGRAPHIC DESIGN: Virginia Pope
PRODUCTION EDITOR: Owen Dugan

For the original edition
SERIES EDITORS: Marc de Smedt and Michel Piquemal

First edition
10 9 8 7 6 5 4 3 2 1

Library of Congress Cataloging-in-Publication Data

Paroles du Tao. English.
The wisdom of Tao/compiled by Marc de Smedt.
p. cm.
Includes bibliographical references.
ISBN 0-7892-0241-7
1. Tao. 2. Taoism. I. Smedt, Marc de, 1946–   . II. Title.
B127.T3P3713 1996
181'.114—dc20   96–21498

The word *Tao* (or *Dao*, according to the new Pinyin transcription of Chinese) actually covers several notions. Literally it means "the Way," but it also means "doctrine," specifically, a collection of moral laws suitable for guiding human behavior. We see the term used for the first time in the *Tao Te Ching*, the classic text of the Way and virtue (or force). Comprising eighty-one chapters and five thousand characters, this work is believed to have been written in the sixth century B.C. by the sage Lao Tzi (or Lao Tzu). It presents the Tao as the essential principle that pre-exists the heavens and the earth, an ineffable, indescribable energy that embraces all things. The Tao creates the Te, that is, force and existence, which amounts to saying that the original void creates or engenders all temporal phenomena.

Founded on this basic tenet and book, Taoism is the overall term used indifferently in the West to define two traditions that are actually distinct by nature. One is philosophical, called the Tao Chia, literally "school of Tao," and the other religious, the Tao Chiao, or "religion of Tao." Throughout China and the rest of Asia the latter has become a popular religion, complete with rites, precepts, ceremonies, exercises for maintaining the health of the body, and sacrifices in honor of the divinities and immortal spirits. Philosophical Taoism, which especially concerns us here, aims to attain inner union with the Tao, hence with the source of all things, making our actions and thoughts conform with our profound nature by practicing various kinds of meditation, and adopting a type of behavior that is spontaneous, simple, and direct.

These two historical traditions have deeply influenced Chinese culture, leaving their mark on medicine, the arts of good government, love, and social interaction, Confucianism, and Ch'an Buddhism, as well as Chinese painting and poetry, both of which directly reflect Taoist principles. One could also argue that despite all the revolutions and evolutions, the spirit of the Tao continues in our day and age to exercise great influence not only over the Chinese people's way of thinking, but also over our own Western modes of being and understanding. We have seen in recent years a rapidly growing number of works on the Tao of psychology, the Tao of management, the Tao of love, and so on, the most famous of these approaches being the *Tao of Physics*, a bestseller by the elementary particle physicist Fritjof Capra. The reason behind this sudden enthusiasm can be ascribed not only to a common need for cerebral exoticism but also to the fact that the concept of the Tao involves a notion that is singularly missing from the Western intellect, that is, the resolution of contradictions and the unity of opposites. This is magnificently represented in Taoism by the image of Yin and Yang, that pair of opposing energies (more and less, day and night, heaven and earth, male and female, and so forth) whose alternating recurrence and interaction constantly give birth to creation. According to the Chinese, it was from these bipolar manifestations that the Five Elements and the Ten Thousand Beings came into existence. We might add that these two fundamental principles are in constant change within each being, just as they are at the heart of the universe. Only by joining them once again are we able to realize the Whole, which, for individuals, means fullness of being.

For us in the West, who are in the habit of opposing tendencies in contradictory terms (Good/Evil, Black/White, and so forth), this philosophy of reconciliation is a concept that is well worth integrating into the structures guiding our thought and behavior. Understanding the Tao amounts to becoming wise.

Marc de Smedt

N.B. For most proper Chinese names, we have used the older Wade-Giles transcription, which is more readily recognized by general readers.